The Fall

Spike T. Adams

Illustrated by John Charlesworth

D1438103

W
FRANKLIN WATTS
LONDON•SYDNEY

Chapter 1

Ricky never did any harm.

But he *was* a loser. No two ways about it.

Carl was always getting at him.

Like that day Ricky held the door open for Kira.

"Ooh, Ricky! You gonna ask Kira out then?" Carl called.

Ricky didn't say a word. He never did.

Just looked at the floor.

But Kira hit back for him.

"You're such a child, Carl. Grow up!"

Me and the others, we were shocked.

The fittest girl in class had just dissed Carl.

And it was coz of Ricky.

There was gonna be trouble.

At morning break Carl told us, "I got a plan."

"What is it?" I asked.

It had to be about Ricky.

Carl grinned. "We're gonna get that freak. Tie him naked to the big tree up at the Outlook..."

The Outlook is this place just outside town.

A cliff top. You can see for miles.

Everyone goes up there after dark.

To get drunk — or get off with each other.

Or both.

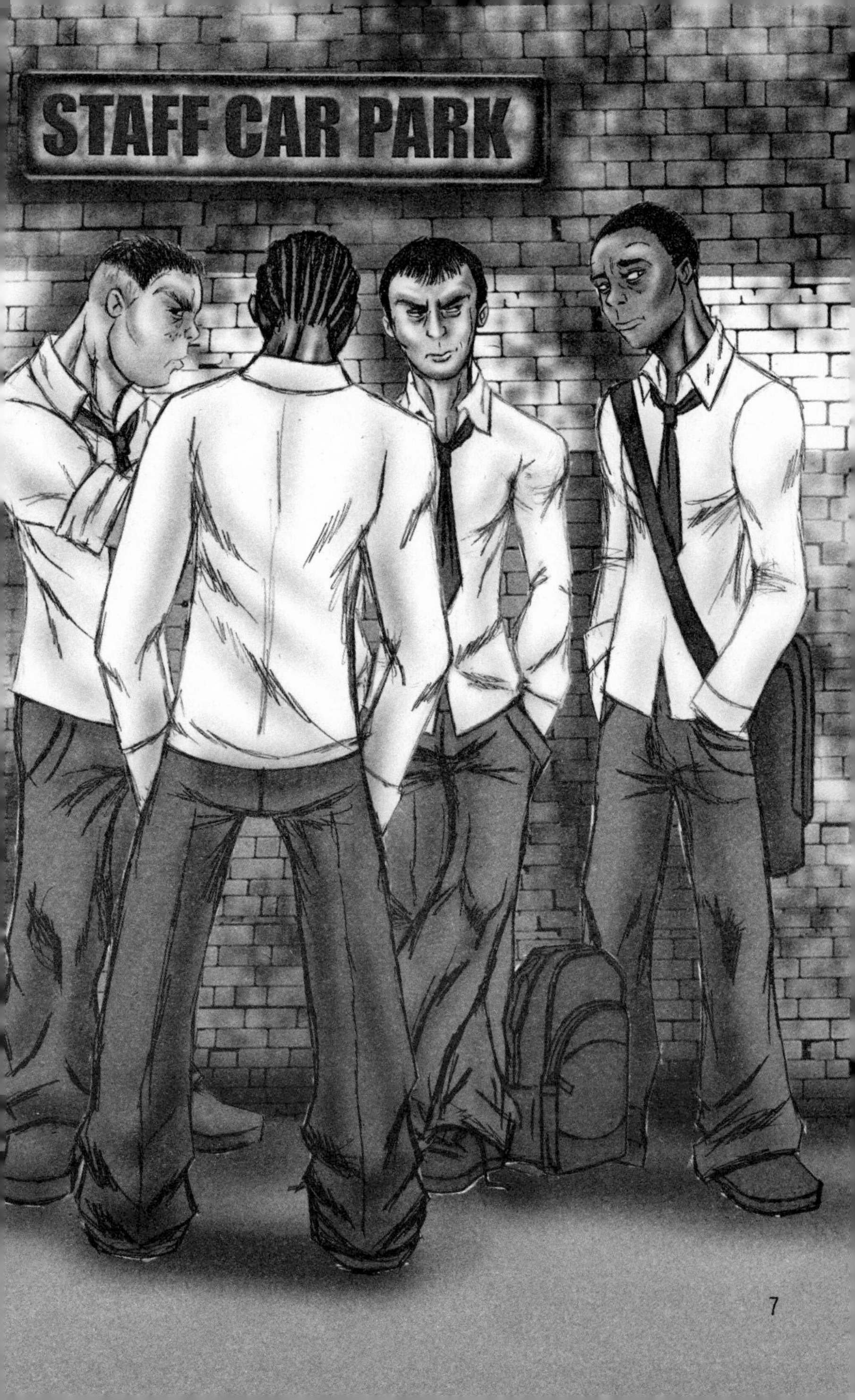
STAFF CAR PARK

"Yeah!" yelled Reese. "When?"

"Tonight," Carl said.

Liam grinned. "Wicked!" he said.

Carl looked at me. "You in, Jon?" he asked.

"Sure," I said.

The plan sounded a bit low to me.

But I was in one of the coolest crews.

And I wanted it to stay that way.

"How we gonna get him up there?" Reese asked.

"I'll show ya," Carl said.

He handed Reese a sheet of paper.

"Write this down," he ordered.

"Dear Ricky,

I'm sorry Carl was so mean to you.

I think you are really great.

Let's hang out at the Outlook tonight.

Meet me there at seven. Kira."

Liam slapped Carl on the back. "Sweet," he said.

Then Carl went and stuffed the note in Ricky's locker.

Chapter 2

Up at the Outlook later, we hid and waited
for Ricky.

There was no one else about yet – too early.

I took a gulp from my can.

"Think he'll show?" I asked.

I really hoped he wouldn't.

Hoped that he'd see the note was a trick.

But no.

There he was.

"Jeez!" Liam hissed. "What does he look like?"

Even I had to smile. Ricky looked a right prick –
still in his school uniform.

Carl took another swig. Picked up the rope.

"Let's do it!" he hissed.

Carl lobbed his can at Ricky.

It only just missed Ricky's head.

Ricky spun round, his eyes wide.

"What you doing out, Pricky?" Carl asked. "Ain't it past your bedtime?"

Ricky held up the note. "I'm meeting Kira," he said.

Liam and Reese fell about laughing.

"That note wasn't from Kira, you sad freak," Carl sneered. "It was from me."

Ricky just stood there, holding the note.

Gutted.

"Get him!" Carl ordered.

Liam and Reese jumped Ricky.

Started ripping off his clothes.

I hung back.

Hoped the others wouldn't see.

"Bastards!" Ricky yelled as he struggled.

"You just wait! I'll..."

Carl, Reese and Liam laughed so loud I didn't hear the rest.

And then Ricky broke free.

Carl went to grab him.

Ricky jumped out of Carl's reach.

He kept on going — away from Carl.

Close to the cliff edge.

And then Ricky tripped.

Like slow motion in a movie, he fell backwards.

Over the edge.

I ran to the edge and looked over.

"RICKY!" I shouted.

It was too dark to see down there.

I called him again. And again.

I don't know how many times.

Nothing.

I turned to look at the others.

"Oh my God!" I shouted. "Look what we've done!"

"We've done nothing — he fell!" Carl snapped.

But he and the others looked as sick as I felt.

"Fell? You shitting me or what?" I screamed back.

Carl grabbed me. He pushed his face right into mine.

"Ricky FELL!" he hissed.

I got my mobile out of my pocket.

"What are you doing?" Carl asked me, eyes all narrow.

"What do you think?" I snapped. "I'm calling for help!"

"You ain't calling anybody," Carl told me.

He snatched my phone and threw it over the Outlook.

And threw Ricky's jumper after it.

Then he picked up the note Ricky had dropped.

Scrunched it up and put it in his pocket.

"Now let's get outta here!" he ordered.

Carl, Liam and Reese began to run down the path into town.

But I ran down to the main road.

There was a phone box there.

The run felt like it took forever.

I grabbed the phone and dialled 999.

I didn't give my name.

"Somebody has fallen," I said. "At the Outlook."

Then I hung up — and started running again.

Chapter 3

That night I got no sleep.

When I closed my eyes I saw Ricky.

The look on his face as he fell...

I put on the TV.

But that didn't help.

Ricky seemed to be there too.

I sat up all night.

Wanting morning to come.

But dreading it.

What would happen then?

Ricky must have been found by now.

Was he telling the police what we did?

Or was Ricky dead?

Morning finally came.

Mum had the local radio station on.

There was nothing about Ricky on the news.

And nothing in Mum's morning paper.

I walked slowly to school.

No police outside.

Liam and Reese were waiting at the gate.

"You seen Carl?" Liam asked me.

"No," I said. "And I don't want to."

Reese rolled his eyes "Shut up, man. We're in the clear."

He leaned right in close to me. "Ricky's OK..."

I stared at them.

"After that fall?" I said. "No way."

Reese shrugged. Then he pointed.

So I looked.

And there was Ricky.

In school.

As if nothing had happened.

31

"Better text Carl," Reese told Liam.

"Tell him there's no trouble - the freak lives on!"

Liam laughed.

I lost it then. "No thanks to you lot!" I hissed.

"You all left Ricky for dead!"

Reese and Liam looked at me open-mouthed.

"Just leave me out of it, from now on," I said.

And I left them to it.

I walked past Ricky, trying not to stare.

But I couldn't help it.

He looked fine.

But how — after such a fall?

It didn't make sense.

Ricky looked back at me.

And then he smiled.

But Ricky never smiled.

It gave me the creeps.

Then he held up a finger and said, "One down."

I had no clue what he meant.

So I shrugged and carried on walking.

Ricky was still a weirdo.

But I was glad he was OK.

Chapter 4

Next day at school there was still no Carl.

And no Liam either.

"Has anyone heard from Carl or Liam?" Mr Travis asked.

No one had.

Reese looked back at me.

I looked the other way.

And saw Ricky looking at me too.

He smiled again. And held up two fingers.

"Two down..." he mouthed.

Did he mean Carl and Liam?

I went cold.

Had Ricky done something to them?

I told myself I'd go up to Ricky.

Confront him.

Ask him what was going on.

But then Reese came rushing over.

He handed me a sheet of paper.

"This was in my locker," he said.

It was a note from Carl.

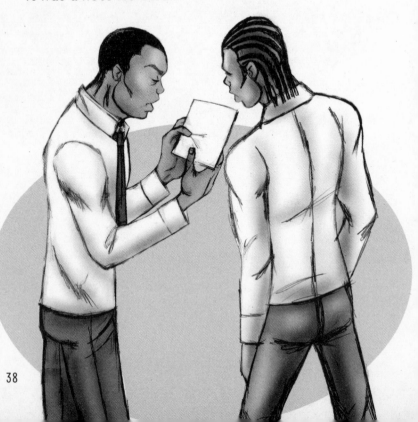

Reese,

We are all in trouble.

Meet me and Liam at the Outlook.

7 o'clock tonight.

We'll find a way out.

Carl

p.s. — better bring Jon.

We got to the Outlook just before seven.

Carl and Liam were there alright.

Bound and gagged.

Hanging.

Eyes wide with fear.

I stood there with Reese.

Couldn't believe what I was seeing.

Carl and Liam tried to speak.

But the tape muffled the sound.

They wriggled like maggots on hooks.

"So you fell for your own trick..." said a voice behind us.

Reese and I swung round.

It was Ricky.

"Shit! What's going on?" Reese shouted.

He waved the note from Carl in the air.

"That note wasn't from Carl, you sad freak," Ricky said, grinning.

"It was from me."

And he laughed.

I'd never heard Ricky laugh before.

He turned his gaze on me.

His eyes full of darkness.

"Glad you could come, Jon," he went on.

And then Ricky swung round and hit Reese.

Hard.

Reese fell to the ground.

Out cold.

Ricky had lost the plot.

Chapter 5

Ricky pulled out a roll of tape from his pocket.

He tore off a strip and taped Reese's mouth.

"Stop it, Ricky!" I pleaded.

I went to pull him off Reese.

But Ricky shoved me away.

I flew back about ten metres.

Crashed into the bushes.

Totally winded.

This was more than weird!

I watched Ricky put Reese over his shoulder.

Like Reese was a sack of feathers.

Then he carried Reese up the tree.

Before long, Reese was hanging with the others.

"Three down!" Ricky crowed. "Or should that be up?"

"Ricky — it was an accident — we called for help!" I pleaded.

"No, Jon," Ricky said. "YOU called for help. Just you."

"How do you know that?" I asked.

"Coz I watched you, Jon," Ricky told me.

"It was already too late."

My blood ran cold as I finally got it.

Ricky had died that night.

Chapter 6

Ricky got down from the tree and came over.

"What's up, Jon?" he asked.

"You look like you've seen a ghost..."

Ricky looked very different now.

His skin was yellow, turning green.

Oozing gashes on his face and hands.

Eyes black and sunken.

Like a dead man walking.

He pointed down into the valley below.

"My body is down there, Jon," he said.

"The police didn't find it. They think your call was a joke."

Ricky swung back up onto the branch.

"Never mind," he went on. "They'll find my body soon."

He took a knife out of his pocket.

"Along with the others."

He started to cut the ropes.

"No!" I screamed. "Ricky don't! It'll make you as low as them!"

Ricky stopped cutting.

He sat there.

Thinking.

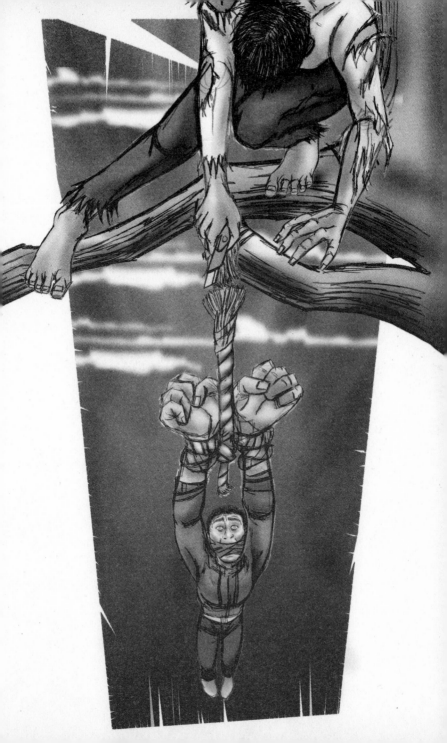

And then he put the knife away.

He took something else out of his pocket.

Threw it to me.

It was my mobile phone.

"There you go, Jon," he said.

"You'd better call for help — coz I ain't getting them down."

He smiled again.

But this time it seemed different.

Real.

Then he leaned sideways.

Let himself fall.

He seemed to sink, slowly, into the darkness.

And was gone.

I looked at my phone.

Flipped it on.

The battery was just about working.

I punched in 999.

As it rang, a strange, ripping noise came from the tree.

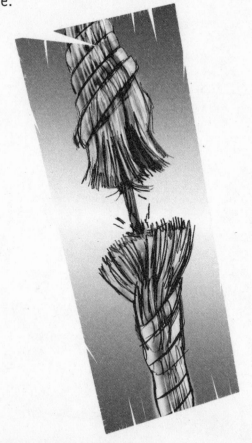

The ropes holding up Carl and the others...

... they were starting to break!

They weren't going to hold for long.

"Come on! Come on!" I shouted at the phone.

And then it beeped.

I looked at the screen.

Low battery.

It went blank.

"Shit!"

I ran for the phone box.

...and I never looked back.

Coz I knew...

...I just knew...

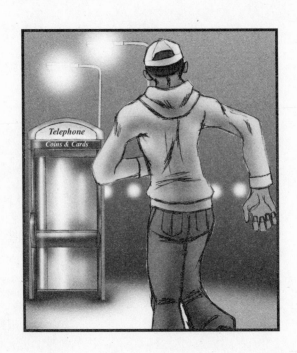

FAST LANE

Jase is on the run.

Dale and his crew are gonna mash him up.

So Tasha takes Jase inside the Hide.

Where he finds out her bloody secret...

978 0 7496 7719 0

More titles by Spike T. Adams:

978 0 7496 7716 9

978 0 7496 7717 6